The Day the Cat Said 'MOO!'

Terrie Sizemore

illustrated by Alenka Trotovšek

The Day the Cat Said 'MOO!;

This is a work of fiction.

Text and Illustrations copyrighted

by Terrie Sizemore ©2024

Library of Congress Control Number: 2022912474

All rights reserved. No part of this book may be

reproduced, transmitted, or stored in an information retrieval

system in any form or by any means,

graphic, electronic, or mechanical without prior written

permission from the author.

Printed in the United States of America

A 2 Z Press LLC

3670 Woodbridge Rd

Deland, FL 32720

bestlittleonlinebookstore.com

sizemore3630@aol.com

440-241-3126

ISBN: 978-1-946908-67-4

Dedication

*Terrie dedicates this to
everyone who needs to
be encouraged to
use their unique voice and
special talents*

This book belongs to :
_____

VINNIE'S VETS
we can fix your pets

The lights are on at Vinnie's Vets,
The sign says 'We can fix your pets!'
But inside, there's trouble brewing,
Instead of purring, this cat is mooing!

And things get worse for Doctor Vin.
A braying hamster's just walked in!
Things around here seem quite wonky,
"This little guy thinks he's a donkey!"

'I've never heard of this before,'
thought Vinnie, looking out the door.
A line of pets lined up round the block,
All waiting there to see the Doc.

Next, in's a little dog called Spot,
Who loudly neighs and starts to trot.
He turns and gallops down the street
In search of sugar lumps to eat.

The Doctor gives his head a scratch.
Why don't the pets and noises match?
The farmer's brought a meowing bull
His sheep's coughed up hairballs of wool!

Says Doctor Vin, "In all the years,
I wouldn't have believed my ears"
His favorite goose rears up and growls.
A group of fieldmice hoot like owls.
The goat crawls in, his tail a-shake,
He's acting like a rattlesnake!

The circus owner's brought his truck,
From inside there's a giant CLUCK.
"Help me Doctor Vin, I beg,
My lion's trying to lay an egg!"

Were great long branches, brown and green,
The biggest nest he'd ever seen!
And up inside a giant nest,
An elephant who tried her best,
To flap her ears and fly away,
Which caused the aged tree to sway.

Doctor Vin's eye's opened wide,
As he saw that elephant inside.
There were neither chicks nor eggs,
But curving tusks and great big legs.
Swishing ears and a trunk of grey,
The great big tree just gave way!
One mighty 'CRACK!' - the tree crashed down,
While off she soared, above the town.

But there was something new, from where it fell,
A strange noise and an unpleasant smell!
It sounded like a croaking frog,
Was hiding in the fallen log.
Then from a hole atop the trunk,
There popped a stinky, stripey skunk!

It gave a 'ribbit,' then hopped off.
And just behind it came a cough.
A chipmunk made a quick escape,
While loudly WHOOPING like an ape.

And lastly from deep inside the tree,
There came a solitary bee.
And then another, soon a swarm,
A cloud of bees began to form!

But no familiar 'BUZZ' was heard,
Instead the bees spelled out a word.
A noise they hadn't heard before,
The bees gave an almighty 'ROAR!'

The skunk plopped in a pond nearby,
As the chipmunk swung on vines up high.
The bees flew off, the crowd perplexed,
And wondered what could possibly be next!

Then, they heard a muffled duck-like sound,
And suddenly from underground,
A little mole with fur of black,
Popped out, looked round, and gave a QUACK!

It waddled round and rubbed its eyes,
But, being blind it's no surprise,
The mole who got into a muddle
Sat paddling in a nearby puddle.

As Doctor Vinnie gave a shout,
"Can anybody help me out?
I need assistance, I confess,
To help me sort out all this mess!"

A loud voice squawked, "I understand,
You need some help - I'll lend a hand"
A huge green parrot, flecked with red,
Swooped in and headed for Vin's head.

"I've had a chat with all these pets,
And know why they're all at the vets.
It's down to how they're seen and heard
by other people" said the bird.

The hamster just wanted to refute,
How people always say, "Aw, how cute!"
He wanted to be strong and tough,
So, like the donkey, he tried to be gruff!"

The lion said "It gets quite boring,
Prowling round the place and roaring,
Roaming plains and scaring men,
No! I think I'll be a mother hen!"

The parrot flew high up in the air,
And gathered all the creatures there.
They came and formed a massive crowd,
Doctor Vinnie cleared his throat and said aloud,

"Everybody has a special voice,
But we all also have a choice!
Hamster - just because you squeak,
It doesn't mean we think you're weak!"

"And bull, you're strong but never do us harm,
relaxing down there on the farm.
You're always useful and not so strange!
And none of you should have to change!"

"And it's the same for all of you,
Dogs should bark, and cows should moo!
Neighing horses, buzzing bees,
And elephants don't live in trees!"

"We all want very much to be heard,
And feel important with each and every word.
We take the words we hear to heart,
And think that we should try and start-

To celebrate ourselves in every way
And take pride in our voice each day.
And know we shouldn't change one bit!
But belt out our exceptional wit."

So everybody is understood
That each of us is just as good.
The sounds we make are all unique,
Quack or trumpet, purr or squeak!

And happy, homeward went the pets,
They owed it all to Vinnie's Vets!
And Doctor Vinnie thanked the bird,
The parrot who helped spread the word!
You be you and I'll be me,
We all bless the world so wonderfully!

The End

All children are special and have their very own and unique voice. The more we try to use someone else's voice, the further we are from who we are meant to be and our own unique and beautiful voice. This little book is to help children see they were meant to have a special voice of their own and to treasure it.

Terrie Sizemore has cherished children's literature for many years. She has taught children most of her life and feels reading is fun and exciting and an invaluable part of every child's life. She hopes every reader enjoys this book as much as she enjoyed creating it.

A2Z Press LLC

A2Z Press LLC published this work. A2Z Press LLC is a publishing company created by Terrie Sizemore for the purpose of publishing literary works by new and aspiring writers. All content is G-rated. We welcome your submissions of ideas for children's literature as well as adult and self-help topics. Science and medicine, holidays and other interesting topics are all welcome. Submit queries to sizemore3630@aol.com or 3670 Woodbridge Rd Deland, FL 32720

Other Books by A 2 Z Press Authors

TV Mouse

There is a Poem Inside of Me

How To Succeed In College

Butterfly Beauties and Magical Moths

Little Leaf Louise

Ants are fANTastic!

Fabulous Frogs and Terrific Toads

Golden Tales: Havoc in Rome

Crabs are Incredible

Fairy Hairy Trouble!

And MORE!

www.ingramcontent.com/pod-product-compliance
Lightning Source LLC
Chambersburg PA
CBHW040003080526
44586CB00027B/2873